THE BASICS OF

PROCESS MAPPING

ROBERT DAMELIO

CRC Press
Taylor & Francis Group
6000 Broken Sound Parkway NW, Suite 300
Boca Raton, FL 33487-2742

© 1996 by Robert Damelio
CRC Press is an imprint of Taylor & Francis Group

No claim to original U.S. Government works
Printed in the United States of America on acid-free paper
15 14 13 12 11 10 9
International Standard Book Number-13: 978-0-527-76316-9 (Softcover)

Library of Congress Cataloging-in-Publication Data

Catalog record is available from the Library of Congress

Visit the Taylor & Francis Web site at
http://www.taylorandfrancis.com

and the CRC Press Web site at
http://www.crcpress.com

Contents

Acknowledgment

When people first discover process mapping, chances are excellent that they will soon come across the work of Geary Rummler (if they haven't done so already). So it was with me some ten years ago, and my professional life has been enhanced dramatically as a result.

I would be doing a disservice to Geary and all other systems thinkers if I did not point out that this book is an introduction to the tool of mapping, and as such represents the tip of the process management iceberg, which is, itself, floating in the "organizations as systems" sea.

Key terminology and the related conventions used in the book, such as cross-functional process map, relationship map, and disconnect owe their origin to Geary. All credit for these important contributions belongs to him.

My purpose with this book is to help spread the word regarding this powerful tool, to add some lessons learned to the evolving story that is mapping, and to perhaps in some small way, thank Dr. Rummler for the profound influence that his work is having on our organizations.

Introduction

Suppose you are planning a cross-country trip by car. One of the first things you might desire is a map to help plan and guide your journey. A current and accurate map helps you plan your route, highlights obstacles and opportunities along the way, provides a way to gauge progress, and helps you communicate and illustrate your intentions to others.

This book is for those who find themselves planning or undertaking a different kind of journey, that of continuous (process) improvement. For your cross-country trip, the path to your destination is some combination of roads, cities, landmarks, and terrain, which is what your map contains. The path for your *improvement* journey consists of the work processes your organization uses to create and transport goods and services to its customers, whether those customers are inside the organization (as in another department, division, site, etc.) or outside the business (someone who purchases or uses your organization's products and services). Thus, the map you use for your improvement journey must focus on the work processes that make up your organization.

Just as there are a variety of maps you may use for your cross-country trip—atlas, state, interstate, city—the same is also true for your improvement journey. This book shows you how to create and interpret three tools that help make work visible: relationship maps, cross-functional process maps, and flowcharts.

Relationship maps show the customer-supplier relationships or linkages that exist between parts of an organization. Though they are most often used to show the big-picture view

Figure 1. Three Views of a Process.

Order Fulfillment Process—Relationship Map View

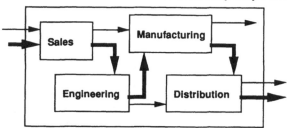

Order Fulfillment Process—Cross-Functional Map View

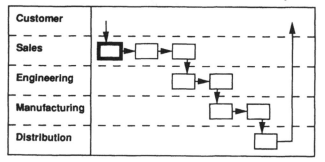

Order Fulfillment Process, "Order taken" step—Flowchart View

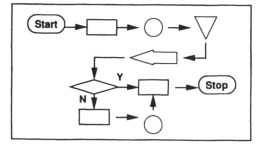

that portrays how the major functions of the business interact with one another, you can draw a relationship map for any level of the organization. The top chart in Figure 1 shows a relationship map of the functions, inputs, and outputs of one organization's order fulfillment process. The flow of the process is shown by the large arrows. The small arrows represent the flow of other work processes.

Cross-functional process maps show how an organization's major work processes cut across several functions. This type of map reveals what goes on inside the black box of the organization's functions, and shows the sequence of steps that make up the work process, as well as the inputs and outputs associated with each process step. You can draw a cross-functional process map for any level of the organization as well. In Figure 1, the middle chart shows a more detailed view of the order fulfillment process. Whereas the relationship map does not generally show the steps that make up a process, this is a key feature of the cross-functional process map. Note that the functions shown in the relationship map are represented by horizontal bands in the cross-functional process map, as is the all-important band which represents the external customer.

Flowcharts are perhaps the best-known tool for illustrating work processes. Flowcharting has long been used to define, document, and analyze processes, particularly at the most detailed level—that of the individual performing the work, or to develop procedures for accomplishing a specific job responsibility. The bottom picture of Figure 1 shows how a flowchart may be used to expand upon the step of "order taken." Note that although this is a single step in the cross-functional process map performed by the sales function, the flowchart portrays the tasks and decisions that a salesperson performs in order to take the customer's order.

Since most readers may already have experience with flow-charts, the main emphasis of this book will be on relationship and process maps. The steps you should follow to create both types of maps are included, as are examples, mapping tips and pitfalls, and checklists to help you evaluate your completed maps.

The following table summarizes many of the key features of each of these three tools.

	Relationship Map	Cross-functional Process Map	Flowchart
Purpose	Shows supplier-customer relationships (which functions or parts of the organization receive inputs from and provide outputs to one another)	Shows functions, steps, sequence of steps, inputs, and outputs for a particular work process	Shows tasks, sequence of tasks, inputs, and outputs for a particular work process
Level of Detail	Least	Medium	Most
Focus	Organization "Context"	Process/People Interface	Process Detail
Key Points	• Does not show processes within or between functions; treats these as a "black box" • Relates pieces of the organization to one another • Shows supplier-customer linkages throughout the organization • Answers the question, "What does the organization provide to its internal and external customers?"	• Shows processes and related steps, inputs, and outputs as well as who performs each step • Reveals what is in the "black box" • Shows supplier-customer linkages for a single process • Answers the questions, "What steps does the organization perform to provide outputs to its internal and external customers? And who performs each step?"	• Shows detailed tasks that make up a process • Does not show who performs the tasks • Does not show supplier-customer linkages • Answers the question, "How does the work actually get accomplished?"

Chapter 1

Why Map a Process?

Maps and flowcharts help make work visible. Increased visibility improves communication and understanding, and provides a common frame of reference for those involved with the work process. Maps are often used to show how work currently gets done in an organization. When used in this way, they represent a snapshot in time that shows the specific combination of the functions, steps, inputs, and outputs that your organization uses to provide value to its customers. Thus, maps and flowcharts help you document your current pathways to customer satisfaction. Analysis of the processes which the maps represent can help you increase customer satisfaction by identifying actions to reduce process cycle time, decrease defects, reduce costs, establish customer-driven process performance measures, reduce non-value-added steps, and increase productivity.

For example, an electrical products distributor created a cross-functional process map of its current incoming material receiving process. The resultant snapshot showed that the receiving process consisted of many more steps than anyone had previously thought, and that few performance measures were currently in place. Each manufacturer had its own way of packing and shipping products. This caused the distributor to adapt its process to each manufacturer, which, in essence, established multiple processes for the same basic function— that of receiving and verifying incoming orders. Examination of the steps within the process showed many to be rework or non-value-added. This prompted the warehouse manager to initiate projects to reduce the non-value-added steps and to establish measures to track timeliness and accuracy of incoming shipment data in order to provide feedback to the manufacturers who shipped the incoming material.

Additionally, maps and flowcharts can be used to show how you *want* work to be done in your organization. By examining a map of current process performance in light of customer requirements and data on sources of customer-perceived value, you can draw a different picture to help you illustrate the pathways you will create to provide value to your customers. Thus maps are also important prerequisites to successful organization design, process reengineering, or benchmarking projects.

In addition to using maps to show how work currently gets done or how you want work to be done, you can also use process maps to:

- Orient new employees.

- Evaluate or establish alternative ways to organize your people to get the work done.

- Quickly get up to speed on what your group, team, or department provides to the rest of the organization and vice versa.

- Identify improvement opportunities.

- Evaluate, establish, or strengthen performance measures.

Using Maps to Orient New Employees

Think back to your first day on the job—any job. What did your boss use to show you how the department fits into the organization, or how your job fits into the department? Chances are it was an organization chart (see Figure 2), and the conversation went something like: "Here's where we are. We report in to the Human Resources organization. My boss is the V.P. of Human Resources, which is the name in this box here. . . ."

Figure 2. Human Resources—Organization Chart.

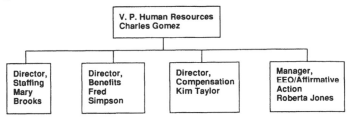

All businesses have organization charts. They are useful tools for communicating reporting relationships, or what is often referred to as the "chain of command." The next time you get a chance to look at one, ask yourself these questions: Where are the customers, or the products or services the organization produces? What work does the organization perform and how does that work get accomplished? These are not idle questions. They are fundamental to success in any business or organization, whether it is manufacturing or service, government or healthcare, large or small.

Here is how you can use process maps to orient new employees. First show them a relationship map of your group, department, or area. This will provide a big-picture view or context that shows how your part of the business relates to others (see Figure 3). Now, the conversation might go like this: "Here is the Human Resources organization. It provides a number of key outputs to the rest of the business. The contribution that we make here in staffing is represented by this box. . . ."

Figure 3. Human Resources—Relationship Map.

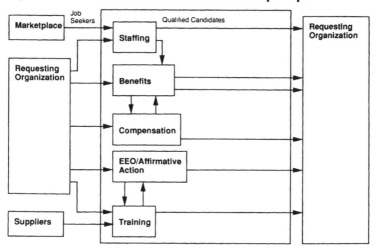

Next, after providing an overview via the relationship map, you could zoom in on the job of your new employee by using a cross-functional process map (see Figure 4). Continue your orientation discussion: "As I said, the contribution that staffing makes is to ensure that positions are filled in a timely and accurate manner. The primary output of staffing is qualified candidates. Your job as recruiter contributes directly to that output via the hiring process."

Figure 4. Hiring Process—Cross-functional Map View.

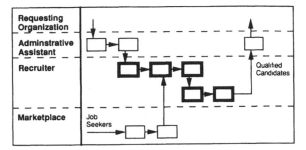

Using Maps to Organize Work

Work gets done by people who are performing one or more steps of a process. This principle allows you to consider various alternatives for accomplishing work by using maps to visualize what a given alternative looks like. Simply put, you can slice a process in many different ways—group the steps that make up one or more processes so that the functions or people required to produce a particular output are on the same team or part of the same work group, for example (see Figure 5). Many organizations are doing this as part of reengineering projects.

Figure 5. Order Fulfillment Process—Alternate Work Groupings.

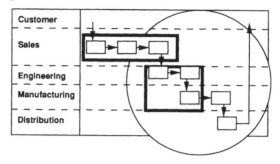

Using Maps to Clarify Roles and Contributions

Suppose you have just taken over a new organization, team, or department. One of your first objectives might be quickly to gain an understanding of the part of the business for which you are now responsible. A relationship map of your organization would provide you with the following information at a glance:

- The outputs (products and services) of your organization.

- The customers for each of those outputs (other parts of the business or other organizations that receive the outputs your organization provides).

- The inputs your organization receives and transforms into outputs.

- The suppliers for each input (other parts of the business or other organizations that provide the inputs your organization consumes or transforms).

- The major functions within your organization that receive and transform each input.

- The links between each function (the connections between the flow of inputs and outputs) within your part of the organization and the critical interfaces your organization has to the rest of the business.

Equipped with this information, you now know with whom you should build or strengthen lines of communication—your customers and suppliers—and at least two things that you should address during that communication—the requirements your customer has for the outputs your organization provides, and the requirements you have for the inputs your suppliers provide to you. You also know the nature of the contribution (the outputs) your part of the business makes to the organization as a whole, as well as the major functions within your business involved in making that contribution.

Using Maps to Identify Improvement Opportunities

Relationship and cross-functional maps can help you discover opportunities to do work better, quicker, and with fewer resources (refer to the section on analyzing maps for more information). Frequently, you may identify significant opportunities for improvement by clarifying the requirements for inputs and outputs, especially if many different functions or parts of the business are involved in producing the final output. Generally speaking, the more handoffs (inputs and outputs that cross functional boundaries) present, the greater the opportunity for improvement. Other opportunities show up in the form of reducing the clutter of the map, for instance, by simplifying a process, or by eliminating redundancies or non-value-added steps, and so on. Maps can also help you establish or assign clear accountability for overall process (rather than department or function) performance by defining the boundaries of the work required to produce a specific output regardless of how many functions or departments the work flow crosses to reach its ultimate destination.

Using Maps to Help Measure Performance

Relationship and cross-functional maps both contain inputs and outputs. In addition, cross-functional maps also show the steps that transform those inputs into outputs. This information helps you evaluate process performance by identifying what to measure and where to measure it, particularly at the enterprise or companywide level.

As a minimum, most quality-conscious organizations seek to measure end-of-process outputs. Process maps make it easy for you to identify these measurement points at a glance. More importantly, cross-functional process maps depict visually the value chain of the organization's major processes. In other words, process A feeds process B and so on, until the final output gets to the external customer. By using maps to illustrate and understand how a given process impacts another process downstream, you can establish a set of measures that can help the entire organization manage its operations in real time, rather than simply relying on a final output measure. This allows you to focus managerial attention on those processes critical to overall operation performance.

Because they show you the steps that make up a process, cross-functional process maps also help you determine where to place in-process measures so that you can assure end-of-output quality by controlling key variables associated with steps in the process while the process is operating. This allows you to prevent defects with your measurement system, rather than merely detecting their presence (see Figure 6).

Each input and output has a set of associated requirements. Once you know what these requirements consist of, you can use that information to construct a set of measures to determine output quality and to assess customer satisfaction. You can measure output quality by focusing on the quality characteristics that cause your customers to value a particular output. To measure customer satisfaction, you must collect customer perceptions data and compare them to the expectations data used to establish input, output, and process requirements. Refer to chapters 5, 7, 8, and 9 of *An Action Guide to Making Quality Happen* (Quality Resources, 1995) for more information on measurement.

Figure 6. Order Fulfillment Process—Measurement Points.

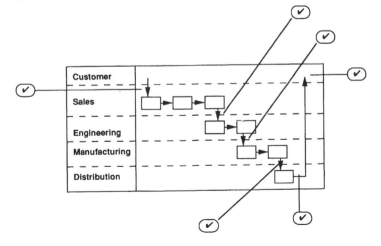

Chapter 2

Flowcharting

A flowchart is a graphic representation of the sequence of steps that make up a process. The author's experience is that the more intelligence built into the flowchart, the greater its usefulness. By intelligence, we mean the use of symbols to represent what actually takes place in the work process. Most users of flowcharts tend to rely on very few symbols and thus limit the tool's usefulness. (It is not the number or variety of symbols that makes the flowchart useful, it is whether you are using enough symbols to help you recognize where waste, delays, rework, and so on occur in a process.) A glance at Figures 7 and 8 on page 17 should help clarify this point.

During the introduction, we mentioned that flowcharting is a tool with which many readers are already familiar. As a result, we will include a list of flowcharting symbols and provide you with a few key points only. You may wish to refer to chapter 4, "Flowcharting: Drawing a Process Picture" in *Business Process Improvement* by H. James Harrington (McGraw-Hill, 1991), or *Cycle Time Reduction: Designing and Streamlining Work for High Performance* by Jerry L. Harbour (Quality Resources, 1996) for more detailed discussions of flowcharts and how they may be used to improve processes. Please be assured that our intention is not to minimize the importance of flowcharts, but rather to emphasize the usefulness of relationship maps and cross-functional process maps since many readers have yet to make use of these powerful tools for process improvement.

FLOWCHARTING SYMBOLS

Here are the symbols you should expect to see in more complete flowcharts.

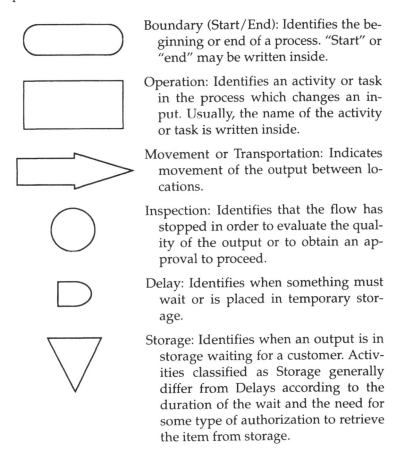

Boundary (Start/End): Identifies the beginning or end of a process. "Start" or "end" may be written inside.

Operation: Identifies an activity or task in the process which changes an input. Usually, the name of the activity or task is written inside.

Movement or Transportation: Indicates movement of the output between locations.

Inspection: Identifies that the flow has stopped in order to evaluate the quality of the output or to obtain an approval to proceed.

Delay: Identifies when something must wait or is placed in temporary storage.

Storage: Identifies when an output is in storage waiting for a customer. Activities classified as Storage generally differ from Delays according to the duration of the wait and the need for some type of authorization to retrieve the item from storage.

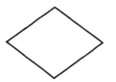

Decision: Identifies a decision or branch point in the process. Write the decision inside. Label each path emerging from the Decision block with the options, such as yes, no, or complete, incomplete, etc.

Document: Identifies when the output of an activity is recorded on paper. Write the name of the document inside.

Database: Identifies when the output of an activity is electronically stored (entered into a database). Write the name of the database inside.

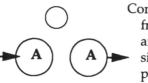

Connector: Indicates that an output from this flowchart will be an input to another flowchart. Write a letter inside the circle to represent the output/input. Sometimes an arrowhead is used along with the circle to denote whether the circle represents an input or an output. An arrowhead pointing at the circle shows that the circle is an output. An arrowhead pointing away from the circle shows that the circle is an input.

Arrows (flow of inputs or outputs): Indicates the sequence and direction of flow within the process and usually the transfer of an output of one activity to the next activity (for which it becomes an input). Use arrows to show movement from one symbol to another.

HOW TO CREATE A FLOWCHART

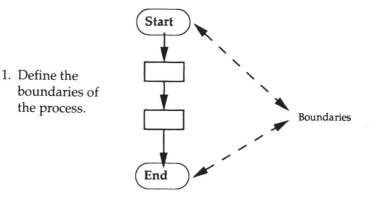

1. Define the boundaries of the process.

2. Keep the flow of the process from left to right and from top to bottom.

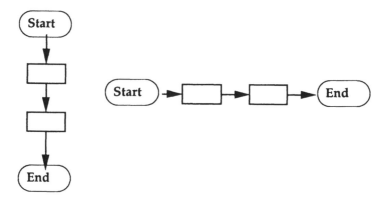

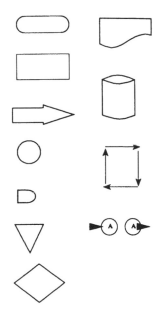

3. Build intelligence into your
   flowcharts; make use of all
   applicable symbols.

4. Keep the symbols at about the same distance
   from one another for ease of interpretation.

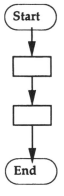

5. Inputs and outputs should pass over and under one another, rather than intersect.

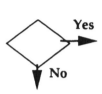

6. Make sure the outputs of your decision symbols are labeled.

Involve those who perform the work when you create the flowchart; if this is impractical, ask them to verify the completed flowchart.

A FLOWCHART EXAMPLE

Consider the two flowcharts below (see Figures 7 and 8). Both illustrate correct applications of the tool, but the second example leads to better analysis of improvement opportunities due to its use of a complete symbol set.

Figure 7. Typical Flowchart.

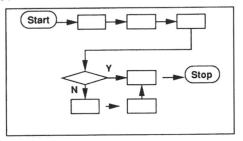

Figure 8. Flowchart with Built-in Intelligence.

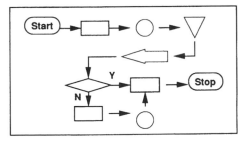

Chapter 3

Process Mapping

COLLECTING THE INFORMATION
NEEDED TO CREATE A MAP

There are three basic methods to collect the process information necessary to create a map:

- Self-generate.
- One-on-one interviews.
- Group interview.

Method 1: Self-Generate

If you already know the work process, you can draw a map
yourself and ask others who work or interact with the process
to react to it. This method produces a map faster than the
other two ways, but its usefulness is limited by the amount of
work process knowledge you possess.

Method 2: One-On-One Interviews

A series of one-on-one interviews with suppliers, performers,
and customers of the work process will enable you to create a
straw model of the process map. You can then route the map
to those you have interviewed and others who are knowledgeable of the process, and ask them to review it for completeness

and accuracy. This method works best when the interviewer has good questioning and listening skills and is able to synthesize information rapidly. It also helps to be familiar with the part of the business that you are mapping before you start the interviews.

Method 3: Group Interview

The third method available to help you create a process map is to arrange for the relevant individuals to participate as a group to generate the map. This method provides the greatest direct interaction among the suppliers, performers, and customers of the work process. A high degree of participation increases the sense of ownership that the group feels regarding the map and, more importantly, the work process. This method works best when a skilled facilitator works with the group to help them identify and lay out the inputs, outputs, and steps of the process. The facilitator does not need to be familiar with the work process. However, he or she should possess strong questioning and listening skills as well as sound knowledge of mapping conventions. (See section on cross-functional process maps.)

TIPS FOR CREATING PROCESS MAPS

- Use the group interview method and a skilled mapping facilitator whenever possible (see "Collecting the Information Needed to Create a Process Map" for more information).

- Select the right people to create the map. Generally speaking, the right people are those who are:
  — Knowledgeable of the process;
  — Interested in improving the process;
  — Available and will stay in the room for the duration.

- Establish ground rules at the start and post them on a flip chart:
  — Map creation method and conventions;
  — No comings and goings;
  — Think rough draft; as author Robert Mager says, "First get it down; then get it good!"
  — Encourage communication;
  — Discourage finger-pointing (no-fault rule applies);
  — Go for quantity of information (breadth versus depth);
  — Keep a bin list (a list of outstanding or unresolved issues).

- Use a room large enough that people can easily move around.

- Have plenty of paper to write on.

- Use Post-it™ Notes to generate initial steps, then categorize information by steps, output, input, measure, function, and so on.

- Sequence and rearrange based on the Post-it™ Notes.

- Consider using a laptop or other computer to record information as you work, especially if you can project the display on a large screen.

- Do not let a particular technology or software package hinder your group process or progress.

- Keep the energy flowing (you know you are successful when people start spontaneously adding or changing items on the map themselves).

- The facilitator should act as a catalyst to jump-start the group and help participants when they stray or start to slow down.

- Respect everyone's contribution.

PROCESS MAPPING PITFALLS

The table below lists typical pitfalls and possible remedies associated with process maps.

Pitfall	Possible Remedy
"Unbalanced" map (too much detail in some areas, not enough in others).	• Compare to other parts of the map; ask, "Does this step contain roughly the same amount of effort as that step?"
Gaps (missing or uncertain steps).	• Ensure that those who help create the map are knowledgeable of the process, or have others review the draft for completeness and accuracy.
Map too "busy."	• Use additional paper and plenty of white space, or expanded maps cross-referenced to base map.
Takes too long, or people getting bogged down.	• Establish ground rules: —outstanding items list —move on after five minutes —follow rough draft principle; first get it down, then get it good —use facilitator.
Unclear terminology, or cannot remember what was said about a particular step.	• Take notes while mapping. • Create glossary.

(continued)

Pitfall	Possible Remedy
Group is mixed (some upper level, some lower levels) or defers to designated decision maker.	• Stress that firsthand knowledge of the work process is what matters. • Strive for equal participation, even if it means redefining the group. • Try to prevent this problem by staffing the group with the right mix up front and explaining to management that they should select those closest to the work.

SELECTING A PROCESS TO MAP

The most important criterion to use to select a process to map—that is, to identify a process to improve—is its impact on customer-perceived value. Specifically, you want the processes that most contribute to customer-perceived value to be world-class or at least competitively superior. Thus, those are the processes that you would benchmark, reengineer, or improve, depending on the current level of process performance as compared to customer expectations and perceptions of the outputs of the process.

Additional criteria that you may use to decide which process to map or which one to map first include:

- Process as part of a core competency.

- Cost reduction.

- Cycle time reduction.

- Defect reduction.

- Bottlenecks.

- Obsolete or changing technology, especially information technology.

- Competitive reasons.

- Mergers or acquisitions.

Chapter 4

Relationship Maps

A relationship map is a picture of the input-output (customer-supplier) connections among parts of an organization, such as functions, departments, divisions, or sites. Relationship maps show:

1. What the organization produces; that is, its products and services—the inputs and outputs shown by arrows.

2. How work flows through functional boundaries—the connections between the arrows and the boxes.

3. Internal or external supplier-customer relationships used to provide or receive products and services—the relationship between the functions represented by the boxes.

Figure 9. Relationship Map.

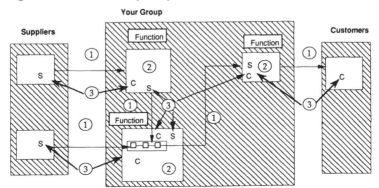

Relationship maps are often used to provide a "high-level" view, similar to an aerial view of the ground below, of functions, inputs, and outputs. Once you have identified something of interest, you then zoom in for a more detailed view, usually via a cross-functional process map.

The steps to follow to construct a relationship map are in the next section.

HOW TO CREATE A RELATIONSHIP MAP

1. Identify the major *outputs* of your group or department.

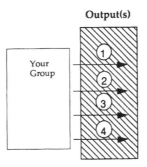

2. Identify your immediate *customers.* These are the customers, internal and external, who first receive your outputs.

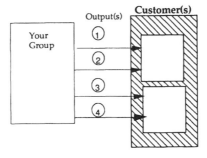

3. List the major *inputs* your group or department requires to produce each major output.

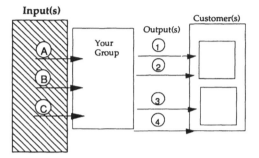

4. Identify where the inputs come from (i.e., who *supplies* them).

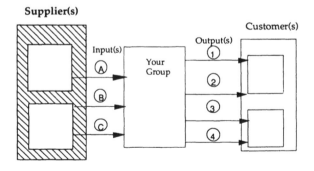

5. What are the major *relationships* (inputs/outputs) *inside* your group or department?

Your Group

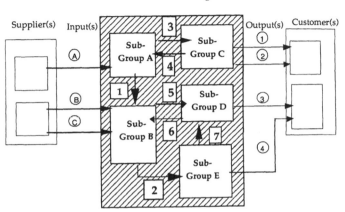

RELATIONSHIP MAP INTERVIEW

The following scene takes place in the office of Phil Greene, the owner of a discount-muffler-style garage. Phil has contracted with Oscar Smith, a quality improvement consultant, to help him better understand garage operations and improve profitability. Oscar is using the one-on-one interview method to generate a relationship map of the garage. Here is a transcript of the interview. The resultant relationship map follows the interview.

Oscar: I need your help in understanding the big picture of the work done here at your garage. In simple terms, what type of work does the garage perform?

Phil: The garage does three main things: we service brakes, mufflers, and shock absorbers. We have one bay in the garage for each type of work.

Oscar: What starts a particular service, such as a muffler replacement?

Phil: We use written work orders for all three services. Nothing happens until there is a work order approved by the customer.

Oscar: What part of the garage is responsible for obtaining the approved work order from the customer?

Phil: Sales. They work directly with the customer. They talk with the customer to figure out what is needed, write the work order, and when the work is done they present the bill to the customer and collect payment.

Oscar: Besides work orders and bills, does Sales have any other forms to complete?

Phil: Yes, they generate material requests and send them to Purchasing. Purchasing uses the material request to generate purchase orders for the various supplies we use.

Oscar: Here's what I've drawn so far. How does it look?

Figure 10. Phil's Garage—Relationship Map.

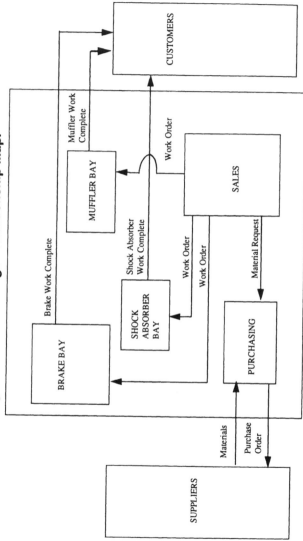

INTERPRETING RELATIONSHIP MAPS

Relationship maps show how the parts of an organization are "wired" together. They can help you better understand who does what to whom; that is, what the supplier-customer links are throughout the organization. Every function, department, or team is always a supplier—it produces one or more outputs—and a customer—it receives one or more inputs from somewhere else. A relationship map helps you quickly identify these supplier-customer connections and answer the following questions:

- Who are the customers for my part of the business?

- What outputs do they receive from me?

- Who are the suppliers to my part of the business?

- What inputs do I receive from them?

- What major functions does my part of the business perform?

- How do the functions in my part of the business "fit in" or contribute to the rest of the organization?

- What are the critical connections (the "interfaces") between my area and the rest of the organization?

Armed with the picture of the business that the relationship map shows, you should determine whether and to what extent the requirements for each input and output are understood between supplying and receiving organizations and are being met. You should also assess how well each critical connection or organizational interface is being managed.

Additionally, you should identify any "disconnects" present on the map. A disconnect is a missing link between an input or output and a function, or a process in a cross-functional process map. They usually show up in one of two ways. First, you may see a function box with no arrows, or not enough arrows (inputs or outputs) coming in or out. The second, and more subtle way to detect a disconnect is to trace the flow of inputs and outputs through functions. If the flow is one way or seems to lead nowhere, it is probably a disconnect. Disconnects are most prevalent in cross-functional processes. The more functions the process crosses, the more disconnects you are likely to find. Major opportunities for quality improvement and cycle time reduction lie in improving and managing these hand-offs between functions.

Figure 11. Phil's Garage—Relationship Map with Interpretation.

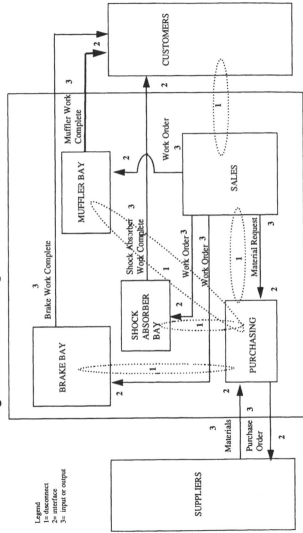

Legend
1 = disconnect
2 = interface
3 = input or output

35

INTERPRETING THE MAP
OF PHIL'S GARAGE

How might you interpret the map of the garage and information you have gained thus far? Consider the following questions as you refer to Figure 11.

1. What disconnects are apparent, if any?

    The map shows the flow of work orders from Sales to the three bays, but no link back to Sales. Recall from the interview script that Sales presents the final bill and collects payment from the customer. The customer receives the outputs of the three bays (e.g., brake work complete) but there is no link shown between the customer and Sales. Materials come from suppliers to Purchasing, but there are no links shown between Purchasing and any of the three bays, nor is there a return link to Sales shown (for example, to provide feedback that the requested material is available, etc.).

2. What are the critical connections or organizational interfaces?

    The two external interfaces are between the garage and its customers and suppliers. Internal interfaces would be between each major function within the garage, such as between the bays and Sales, or Sales and Purchasing.

3. What are the major inputs and outputs?

    Work orders, purchase orders, materials, material requests, brake work complete, muffler work complete, shock absorber work complete are examples of major inputs and outputs.

4. What are the requirements for each input and output?

    The interview does not provide us with this information.

5. Do any other questions come to mind based on the information provided in the interview or from reviewing the completed map?

    What happens to the payment collected by Sales from the customer? How do suppliers get paid for the materials they provide? Do the three bays work with each other in any way? Do they share information? What information is needed on a work order for work to begin? How do you know that the work each bay performs is correct?

You may have identified other questions and disconnects. Does that mean that this map is incorrect or useless? Not at all. What it demonstrates is that you should not expect the first map you draw to be complete and accurate. Maps often begin as rough drafts. Next, the draft should be reviewed by those closest to the work process for completeness and accuracy. Finally, the map may be redrawn to lay out functions better so that inputs and outputs do not cross so many lines.

Chapter 5

Cross-Functional Process Maps

Cross-functional process maps illustrate how work gets done in organizations—the paths that inputs follow as they get transformed into outputs that customers value. They show the steps that make up a process, as well as:

1. Inputs and outputs of each step.

2. Sequence of steps.

3. People, functions, or roles that perform each step.

Figure 12. Cross-Functional Process Map.

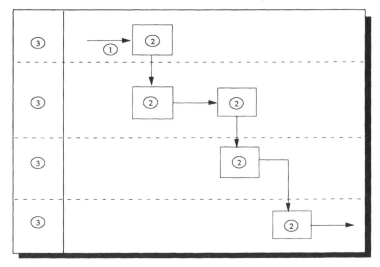

Use the following mapping conventions:

1. Use a box to show the steps that make up the process. Shade the box if you have a separate map or flowchart of this step.

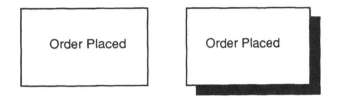

2. Draw a line with an arrowhead to show an input or an output associated with each step. Label the inputs and outputs. This helps with subsequent analysis so that you can clearly see the transformation or value being added by each process step.

3. Keep general left-to-right sequence of converting inputs into outputs.

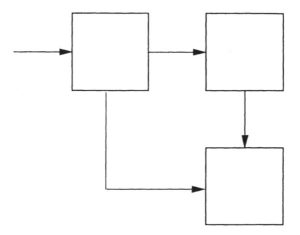

4. Inputs and outputs should pass over and under one another, rather than intersect.

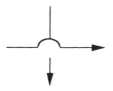

5. Use the diamond symbol to indicate a decision.

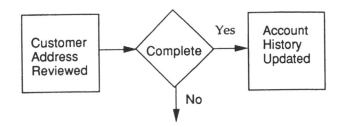

6. Draw horizontal bands using dotted lines to represent the functions, departments, and roles crossed by the work process. Inputs and outputs pass through these bands.

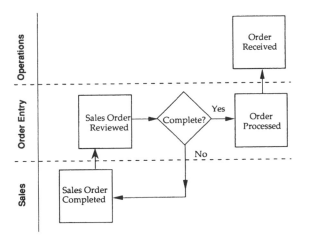

7. When several functions jointly perform the same step (e.g., Review Account), draw the box so that it includes all the functions involved. Solid lines show shared involvement. Dotted lines show that one or more functions is *not* involved with the activity. Here, customer history is reviewed by functions A, B, and C.

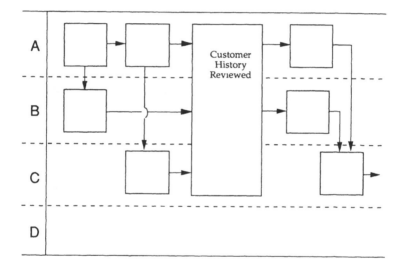

Next, customer history is reviewed by functions A, B, and D. Function C is not involved.

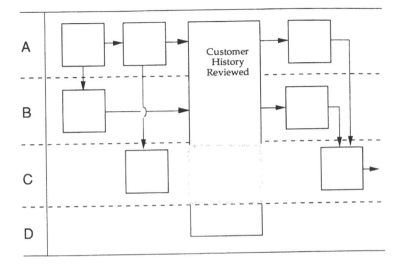

8. Split the band if you want to show a subset of a function (e.g., Sales).

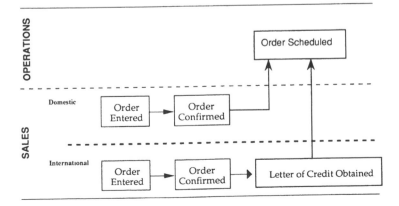

HOW TO CREATE A CROSS-FUNCTIONAL PROCESS MAP

1. Place a large (at least 3' × 6') piece of paper on a wall or flat surface.

2. Draw one horizontal band for each function involved in the process. Bands may also be used to represent roles, such as manager, or job titles, such as production supervisor. If the process involves only one function, skip this step.

3. Label the functions, starting with the customer (internal or external) at the top, and then the functions closest to the customer.

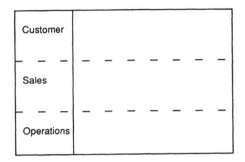

4. Ask each group member to write on Post-it™ Notes the steps that make up their function's portion of the process, and place the Post-it™ Notes on the map.

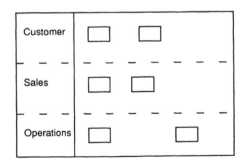

5. Resequence the Post-its™ until the group is satisfied that the process is accurately mapped.

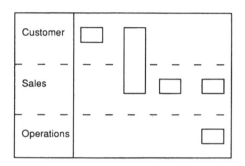

6. Add and label all inputs and outputs to complete the map.

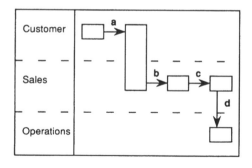

CROSS-FUNCTIONAL PROCESS MAP
INTERVIEW

The following is a continuation of the discussion between Phil Greene and Oscar Smith which began on page 30. There have been no adjustments or changes to the relationship map (Figure 10) that first appears on page 32.

Oscar: Let's take a closer look at the work that takes place in the muffler bay. Based on the information from our earlier session, here is what I understand so far. A customer drives in and speaks with someone in Sales. After Sales and the customer have discussed the work to be done, Sales writes a work order and asks for the customer's approval. Is that right, so far?

Phil: Yes.

Oscar: What happens next?

Phil: Sales gives the work order to the technician, who reviews it and prepares to start the job.

Oscar: What does the technician do?

Phil: He pulls a new muffler from inventory. Then, he removes the old muffler. Next, he installs the new muffler. Then, he starts the car, and checks for leaks and the proper exhaust. If everything is OK, he turns off the car, and notifies Sales that the job is complete. If the job is not OK, he begins troubleshooting by double-checking the clamps, seals, and so on.

Oscar: Once Sales is notified by the technician, they pre-
pare the bill for the customer and collect payment,
right?

Phil: Right.

Oscar: Can you think of anything else that takes place as
part of a muffler replacement?

Phil: Not right now. I think we've about covered it.

Oscar: Let's take a look at the map of the muffler replacement process.

Figure 13. Muffler Replacement Process—Cross-Functional Process Map.

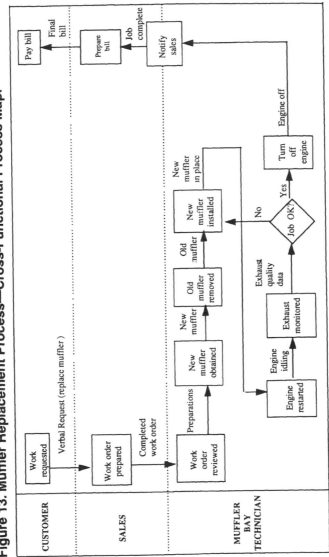

INTERPRETING CROSS-FUNCTIONAL PROCESS MAPS

Cross-functional process maps show the value-producing chains of the business. They also depict the pathways to customer satisfaction.

Whereas relationship maps focus more on the big-picture supplier-customer links that make up a business, cross-functional process maps show us in more detail *how* an organization uses processes to create value for its customers.

Cross-functional process maps answer the questions:

- What steps are required to produce a particular output?

- What is the order in which the steps are performed?

- Who (which function) performs each step?

- What are the handoffs or interfaces between functions?

- In what parts of the process do the handoffs occur?

- What are the inputs required and the outputs produced at each step of the process?

Like relationship maps, cross-functional process maps often contain disconnects (missing or deficient inputs or outputs). Since cross-functional maps show what takes place inside one or more functions for a particular process, any disconnects that were present in the relationship map of those functions will also be present here.

As you review your map, you may discover inputs or outputs that do not feed into any other steps within the same function, nor into steps within other functions. You may also find missing or implied steps, inputs, or outputs. Each of these is a form of disconnect that should be noted and resolved.

Figure 14. Muffler Replacement Process—Cross-Functional Process Map with Interpretation.

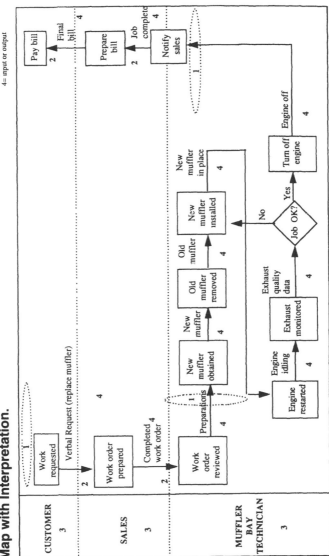

Legend
1 = disconnect
2 = interface
3 = process performer
4 = input or output

51

INTERPRETING THE MAP OF THE MUFFLER REPLACEMENT PROCESS

How might you interpret the map of the muffler replacement process and the information you have gained thus far? Consider the following questions as you refer to Figure 14.

1. What disconnects are apparent, if any?

   Implied or missing steps might include: drive car into muffler bay, return car to customer, obtain or verify needed supplies and tools, and accumulate old mufflers for recycling. Implied or missing outputs might be: car in place at muffler bay, car in place at parking lot, supplies and materials, old muffler, and payment.

2. What are the critical interfaces in the process, and where do they occur?

   The critical interfaces are between Sales and the customer, and Sales and the muffler bay technician.

3. Who performs each step of the process?

   By reading each band horizontally, you can determine this information at a glance. The customer requests the work and pays the bill. Sales completes the work order, receives notification that the job is complete, and prepares the final bill. All other steps are performed by the muffler bay technician.

4. What are the inputs required and outputs produced at each step of the process?

   The major inputs, those at the start of the process, are the verbal request from the customer and the completed work order from Sales. Major outputs, those at the end of the process, are the completed job and the final bill. Additional inputs required to complete the job are preparations, new muffler, old muffler, new muffler in place, engine idling, exhaust quality data, and engine off.

5. What are the requirements for each input and output?
   The interview does not provide us with this information.

6. What additional questions might you ask?
   How does the car get to the muffler bay? Who performs this step? How is the car returned to the customer? Who performs this step? What happens to the payment made by the customer? What tools or supplies does the technician need to perform each step of the process? Where do these inputs come from?

You may have identified additional disconnects or questions. Like the relationship map of the garage, it is apparent that additional information is required to produce a complete and accurate map of the muffler replacement process. To obtain the additional information, you should review the map with representatives of each function involved with the muffler replacement process. Better yet, try to observe the muffler replacement process as it is being performed.

Chapter 6

Analyzing a Process

Initial analysis of a process begins with interpreting the completed maps. (See sections on interpreting relationship and cross-functional process maps.)

Subsequent process analysis most often requires that you collect or obtain process performance data, such as cost, time, or defect data. The particular type of analysis is usually determined by the type of project you are working on and the reason the process was selected to be mapped or improved.

For example, suppose you are working on a quality improvement project, and the work process was selected because of customer complaints regarding errors on the process output. In this case, you might collect and analyze defect data in order to determine and eliminate the root causes of the defects. Alternatively, if the customer was complaining that the output took too long to receive, you would concentrate on cycle time analysis, rather than defects, assuming that the outputs are defect-free.

Regardless of any other subsequent analysis you will perform, once you have reviewed and interpreted a completed map or flowchart, you should ask the group to classify each step as value-added or non-value-added, since elimination of non-value-added steps always reduces cycle time and cost and increases productivity.

According to the authors of *The Reengineering Handbook* (Mangelli and Klein, AMACOM Books, 1994), a value-added step usually has three characteristics:

- It accomplishes something the *customer* cares about.

- It transforms (physically changes) an input.
- It is important to do it right the first time.

The important thing to remember is that maps are means, not ends. Often, but not always, one or more steps of the process that you mapped will require a more detailed breakdown before you are able to recommend improvements.

The following pages show how each of the three tools—Relationship Maps, Cross-functional Maps, and Flowcharts—may be used in a variety of performance improvement applications. They contain the information listed below for each improvement application.

Typical analysis questions: This is a "thought-starter" list of the questions to be answered as part of the analysis. They are representative and by no means the only ones that will arise.

Additional data required: Generally speaking, maps do not provide the process performance data needed for subsequent analysis. This section lists the type of data required for a particular application.

Tool used: Some combination of the following three tools will be used for each application: Relationship Maps, Cross-functional Process Maps, or Flowcharts.

Map portions used: These are the specific parts of the maps that are most relevant to the particular analysis.

Analysis methods: These are the methods of analysis that are likely to be most useful for the specific application, and for which the process maps provide the foundation.

Application: Cost Reduction

Typical Analysis Questions:

- What does it cost to operate the process?

- Which steps cost the most? Why?
- Which steps add value and which do not?
- What are the causes of cost in this process?

Additional data required:
- Cost for each input, output, and step
- Determination of whether the step is value-added or non-value added

Mapping Used:
- Cross-functional Process Map
- Flowchart

Map Portion Used:
- Inputs
- Outputs
- Steps

Analysis Methods
- Pareto charts
- Activity-based costing
- Activity-based management

Application: Cycle Time Reduction

Typical Analysis Questions:
- Which steps consume the most time? Why?

- Which steps add value and which do not?
- Which steps are redundant, bottlenecks, or add complexity?
- Which steps result in delays, storage, or unnecessary movement?

Additional data required:

For each step determine:

- Elapsed time
- Whether the step is value-added or non-value-added
- Complexity
- Redundancy
- Bottleneck
- Delays
- Storage
- Transportation

Mapping Used:

- Cross-functional Process Map
- Flowchart

Map Portion Used:

- Steps

Analysis Methods

- Pareto charts
- Work simplification

Application: Quality Improvement (defect reduction)

Typical Analysis Questions:

- Is variation due to common or special causes?
- What are the causes of the defects?
- Which variables must be managed to have the desired effect on the relevant quality characteristics?
- How should the process be changed to reduce or eliminate variation?

Additional data required:

- Process requirements
- Common or special causes of variation
- Desired quality characteristics
- Defect categories and descriptions

Mapping Used:

- Cross-functional Process Map
- Flowchart

Map Portion Used:

- Inputs
- Outputs
- Steps

Analysis Methods

- Statistical methods
- Pareto charts
- Cause & effect
- Root cause analysis
- Design for manufacturability
- Design of experiments

Application: Measurement System Design or Evaluation

Typical Analysis Questions:

- Based on customer expectations data, what are the requirements for the inputs and outputs of this process?
- What should our measures be to assure that the requirements are met?
- Do our current measures assess what is important to our customers?
- What happens to the measurement data we currently collect?

Additional data required:

- Process requirements

Mapping Used:

- Relationship Map

- Cross-functional Process Map
- Flowchart

Map Portion Used:

- Inputs
- Outputs

Analysis Methods

- Measurement system analysis

Application: Customer Satisfaction Measurement

Typical Analysis Questions:

- How does process performance data compare to customer expectations and perceptions data?

Additional data required:

- Customer expectations data
- Customer perceptions data
- Process performance data

Mapping Used:

- Relationship Map
- Cross-functional Process Map
- Flowchart

Map Portion Used:

- Inputs
- Outputs

Analysis Methods

- Market research
- Stratification: grouping data by categories and looking for patterns in the data
- Comparative analysis

Application: Horizontal Management

Typical Analysis Questions:

- Who should be accountable for end-to-end process performance?
- How can we structure the organization to manage processes in addition to functions?

Additional data required:

- Customer expectations data
- Customer perceptions data
- Process requirements data

Mapping Used:

- Relationship Map
- Cross-functional Process Map

Map Portion Used:

- Inputs
- Outputs

Analysis Methods

- Organization design or analysis

Application: Benchmarking

Typical Analysis Questions:

- What are the best-in-class practices, metrics, and enablers?

- What are the root causes of superior process performance?

- What makes a given practice so effective?

- Why is one measure (metric) preferable to another?

- Why is the process configured (designed) to operate this way?

Additional data required:

- Practices (your own process plus those of the benchmark partners)

- Metrics (your own process plus those of the benchmark partners)

- Enablers (your own process plus those of the benchmark partners)

Mapping Used:

- Cross-functional Process Map
- Flowchart

Map Portion Used:

- Inputs
- Outputs
- Steps

Analysis Methods

- Comparative analysis

Application: Reengineering

Typical Analysis Questions:

- How can the function of this process be performed differently?
- How can we make the process more effective, efficient, and adaptable?
- How can we add value while reducing cost?
- What will the jobs in the new process consist of?
- How can we use information technology to empower job performers?

Additional data required:

- Cost of each input, output and step

- Elapsed time
- Customer satisfaction
- Number of persons operating process
- Information systems
- Process requirements
- New job tasks

Mapping Used:
- Cross-functional Process Map
- Flowchart

Map Portion Used:
- Inputs
- Outputs
- Steps

Analysis Methods
- Any or all of the preceding

Further Reading

An Action Guide to Making Quality Happen, Robert Damelio and William Englehaupt, Quality Resources, 1995.

The Basics of Benchmarking, Robert Damelio, Quality Resources, 1995.

Business Process Improvement, H. James Harrington, McGraw-Hill, 1991.

Cycle Time Reduction, Jerry Harbour, Quality Resources, 1995.

Improving Performance: How to Manage the White Space on the Organization Chart, 2nd ed., Geary A. Rummler and Alan P. Brache, Jossey-Bass, 1995.

Keeping Score: Using the Right Metrics to Drive World-Class Performance, Mark Graham Brown, Quality Resources, 1995.

The Process Reengineering Workbook: Practical Steps to Working Smarter and Faster Through Process Improvement, Jerry L. Harbour, Ph.D., Quality Resources, 1995.